Baluchitherium

Diplodocus

Tyrannosaurus

British Library Cataloguing in Publication Data
Baglio, Bennett
    Dinosaurs.
    I. Title   II. Robinson, Bernard
    567.9'1   QE862.D5
    ISBN 0-7214-1078-2

Published by Ladybird Books Ltd Loughborough Leicestershire UK
Ladybird Books Inc Lewiston Maine 04240 USA
© LADYBIRD BOOKS LTD MCMLXXXVIII

Printed in England

Dinosaurs

Adapted by Ben M Baglio
from Colin Douglas's original text
Illustrated by B H Robinson

Ladybird Books

Once the Earth was very hot. As
it slowly cooled, rain began to fall.
The rain water made rivers and

oceans. Nothing lived on the land
or in the sea. There were no
plants, no animals and no people.

Life began in the sea

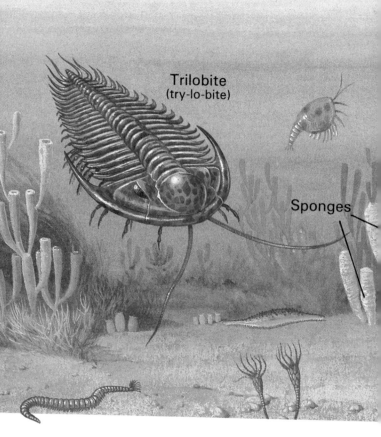

Trilobite
(try-lo-bite)

Sponges

The first plants were *algae* and the
first animals were tiny creatures
called *protozoa*. Over millions of
years, the animals changed into

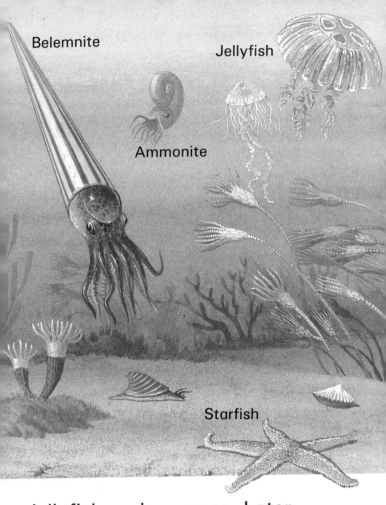

Belemnite

Jellyfish

Ammonite

Starfish

jellyfish and sponges. Later,
there were worms and starfish.
Later still, there were animals
that had shells.

The age of fish

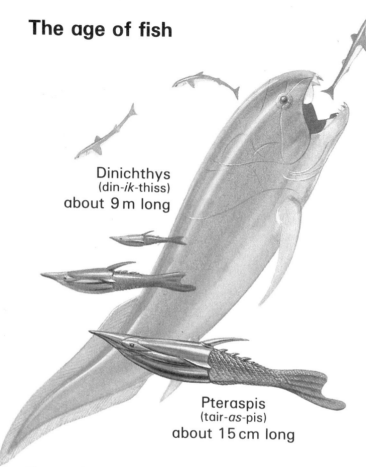

Dinichthys
(din-*ik*-thiss)
about 9 m long

Pteraspis
(tair-*as*-pis)
about 15 cm long

Bony-headed fish like these
began to live in the sea. Most,
like Pteraspis, were quite small,
but Dinichthys was as long as a
bus!

At this time, plants began to grow on the land. They looked like the mosses and ferns we see today, but some were as tall as trees.

Onto the land

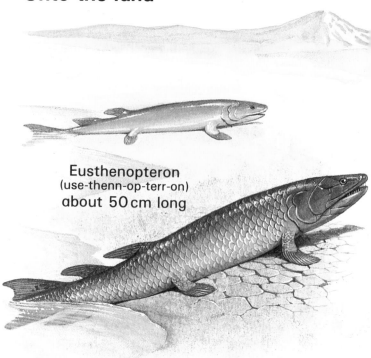

Eusthenopteron
(use-thenn-op-terr-on)
about 50 cm long

Slowly, the Earth's climate
became hotter again, and many
lakes and rivers dried up. Some
fish, like Eusthenopteron, grew
lungs and very strong fins so that
they could crawl onto the land.

The first amphibians (am-fib-y-ans)

Ichthyostega
(ik-thee-o-*stee*-ga)
about 1 m long

Millions of years later, some fish grew legs. They had become amphibians. This means that they could live both on land and in water.

Eryops
(*air*-ee-ops)
about 2 m long

As time went by, many different kinds of amphibians appeared. Some were only 5 cm long. Others, like Eogyrinus, grew as long as 4.5 m.

Eogyrinus
(a-o-jy-ryne-uss)
about 4.5 m long

Amphibians ruled the Earth for
many millions of years. But as
the climate became drier, slowly,
some amphibians changed into
reptiles.

The first reptiles

Seymouria
(see-*more*-ee-ya)
about 60 cm long

Unlike amphibians, reptiles do
not need to go into water to lay
eggs. The females lay waterproof
eggs on land. Seymouria was
one of the first reptiles.

Edaphosaurus
(ee-daff-o-*sor*-uss)
nearly 3 m long

Reptiles began to look less like
amphibians. Some, like
Edaphosaurus, grew large fins on
their backs. These fins could be
up to 2 m high.

Dimetrodon
(di-*mee*-trow-don)
about 3 m long

Dimetrodon was one of the first
reptiles to eat meat. It ate
smaller amphibians and reptiles.

An amphibian and a reptile of today

Frog

Alligator

There are still reptiles and amphibians on Earth today. The frog is an amphibian. It lays its eggs in water. The alligator is a reptile. It lays its eggs on land.

Sea reptiles

Ichthyosaurus
(ik-thee-o-*sor*-uss)
between 3 and 12 m long

Some reptiles went back to live in the water. They did not lay eggs. The young sea reptiles hatched from eggs *inside* the mother's body.

Plesiosaurus
(pless-i-o-*sor*-uss)
about 12 m long

Ichthyosaurus looked like a dolphin
and could swim very fast to catch
fish to eat. Plesiosaurus could not
swim fast. Its very long neck
helped it to find food.

Gliding reptiles

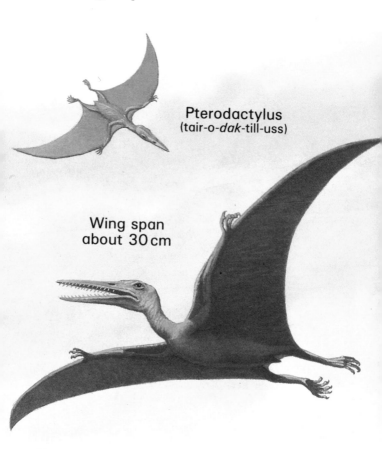

Pterodactylus
(tair-o-*dak*-till-uss)

Wing span
about 30 cm

Some reptiles grew wings which
were made of a thin layer of
skin. These let them glide
through the air. Some of these

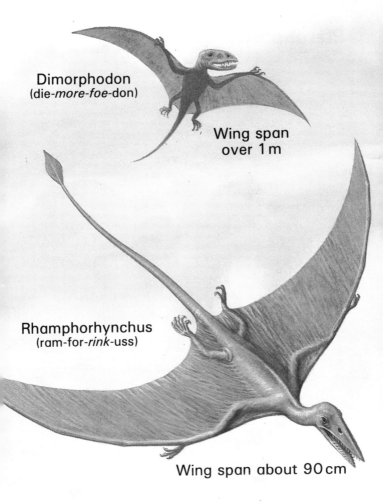

Dimorphodon
(die-*more-foe*-don)

Wing span
over 1 m

Rhamphorhynchus
(ram-for-*rink*-uss)

Wing span about 90 cm

reptiles were enormous, but
many were no larger than a
small bird. Gliding reptiles ate
fish or small reptiles and insects.

Pteranodon
(tair-ran-o-don)

Pteranodon was one of the
biggest gliding reptiles. Its wing
span could be as wide as 8 m.
Gliding reptiles lived on cliffs
near the sea.

Wing span
up to 8 m

23

Footprints from the past

Very large bones were found in England during the 1820s. Later, huge footprints were found both in England and in America.

Skeleton of Apatosaurus

The footprints and bones were those of a dinosaur. They had been buried in the ground and *preserved* for millions of years.

The word dinosaur means ''terrible lizard''.

25

Diplodocus and Apatosaurus

There were many kinds of
dinosaurs, and they all lived long
before the first humans. Some
were very small and quick, but
others were very big and slow.

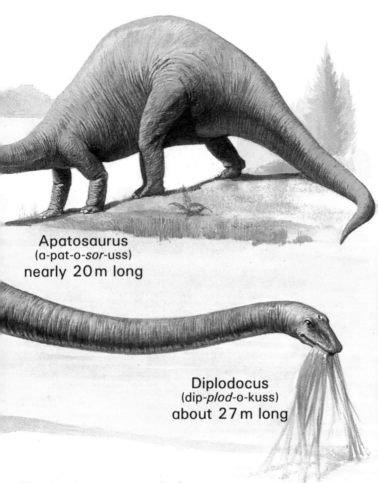

Apatosaurus
(a-pat-o-*sor*-uss)
nearly 20 m long

Diplodocus
(dip-*plod*-o-kuss)
about 27 m long

Diplodocus and Apatosaurus
were two of the biggest
dinosaurs. They were gentle
plant-eaters and lived in herds for
protection.

Stegosaurus and Allosaurus

Stegosaurus
(stĕg-o-*sor*-uss)
about 6 m long

Stegosaurus was very slow. It
had bony plates and a spiked tail
to protect it from its enemies.

Allosaurus
(al-lo-*sor*-uss)
over 9 m long

Allosaurus was a large meat-eating dinosaur that stood on two legs. Its mouth opened so wide that it could swallow small animals whole.

Hypsilophodon and Iguanodon

Hypsilophodon
(hip-sill-loff-o-don)
up to 2 m long

Hypsilophodon was a very small
dinosaur but it could move
quickly on two legs to escape
from its enemies.

Iguanodon
(ig-*wan*-o-don)
over 9 m long

Iguanodon was a much larger
plant-eater. It had a bony spike
on each thumb that it used to
fight off its attackers.

Polacanthus
(poll-a-kan-thuss)
about 4 m long

Remains of Polacanthus were
found in England. The double
row of spikes on its back and the
bony plates on its tail kept other
animals away.

Ankylosaurus

(an-*kile*-lo-*sor*-uss)
over 4.5 m long

Ankylosaurus appeared on Earth
later than Stegosaurus. Its body
was covered with bony plates.
At the end of its tail was a big
lump of bone with spikes, which
Ankylosaurus used as a club.

Anatosaurus and Corythosaurus

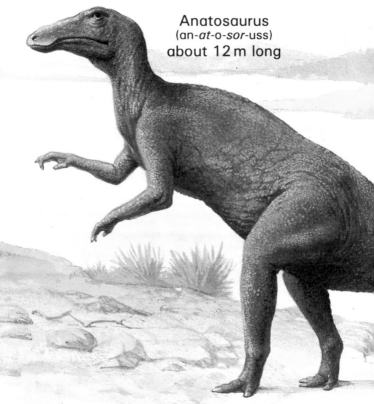

Anatosaurus
(an-*at*-o-*sor*-uss)
about 12 m long

These two dinosaurs are known
as ''duck bills'' because they had
bills or beaks that were broad
and flat, just like a duck's. They
had many rows of teeth for

Corythosaurus
(cor-ith-o-*sor*-uss)
about 9 m long

grinding tough plants.
Corythosaurus had a bony crest
on its head that looked like a
helmet. Its name means "helmet
reptile".

Protoceratops

(pro-toe-*sair*-a-tops)
nearly 2 m long

Protoceratops had a tough bony collar to protect its neck.

Fossil eggs have been found in Mongolia with the bones of baby Protoceratops inside. Each egg was about 20 cm long.

Styracosaurus

Styracosaurus
(sty-rak-o-*sor*-uss)
about 4.5 m long

Styracosaurus looked fierce but
it ate plants, not other animals.
It had a beak like a parrot's and
long spikes on its head.

Tyrannosaurus

Tyrannosaurus
(ty-ran-no-*sor*-uss)
about 12 m long

Tyrannosaurus was the largest and fiercest meat-eating dinosaur. Its jaw was over 1 m long and its teeth were 15 cm long.

Monoclonius and Triceratops

Monoclonius
(mon-o-*klon*-ee-uss)
about 6 m long

Dinosaurs roamed the Earth for nearly 150 million years. These were two of the last dinosaurs to appear. Triceratops was a plant-eater. It was very big and had two horns above its eyes.

Triceratops
(try-*ser-a*-tops)
about 9 m long

Male Triceratops may have used these horns to fight, as male deer do today.

The first birds

Archaeopteryx
(ar-kee-*op*-terr-iks)
Wing span
about 40 cm

Archaeopteryx was the first bird.
It lived at the time of the
dinosaurs and was about the size
of a magpie.

Archaeopteryx had teeth like a
reptile's. Its long bony tail had
feathers growing on it and its
wings had claws.

The first mammals

Phascolotherium
(fas-kol-o-theer-ee-um)
about 20 cm long

A mammal is an animal that is
covered with fur and feeds on its
mother's milk when it is young.
The first mammals lived at the
time of the dinosaurs and the
first birds.

Megatherium
(mega-theer-ee-um)
about 5.5 m high

Early mammals, like
Phascolotherium, were no larger
than mice or rats. Later, some
mammals became much bigger.
Megatherium was about 5.5 m
high. It lived in South America.

45

More mammals

Uintatherium
(oo-in-ta-theer-ee-um)
about 3.5 m long

Uintatherium was as big as an
elephant. It looked fierce, but it
ate only plants.

Baluchitherium
(bal-oo-ki-theer-ee-um)
about 8 m high

Baluchitherium was the tallest
land mammal that has ever lived.
It was about 8 m tall – more than
three times as high as a man,
and it ate leaves and twigs.

Eohippus
(ee-o-hip-puss)

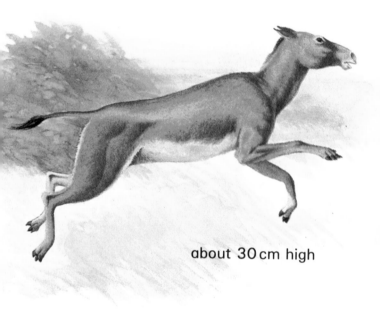

about 30 cm high

Eohippus was the earliest
ancestor of today's horses and
zebras. It was only 30 cm high
and lived in the forests. Although
it had toes instead of hooves, it
could still run very fast.

Coelodonta
(see-lo-don-ta)

about 2.5 m long

In the Ice Ages, thousands of
years ago, much of the Earth
was covered in snow and ice.
Many types of mammals died of
the cold. But Coelodonta, the
woolly rhinoceros, had a long,
hairy coat to keep it warm.

Woolly mammoth

about 3 m high
at shoulder

The woolly mammoth was like a
huge elephant with a hairy coat.
It lived during the Ice Ages. The
first humans hunted mammoths
for food.

Sabre-toothed tiger

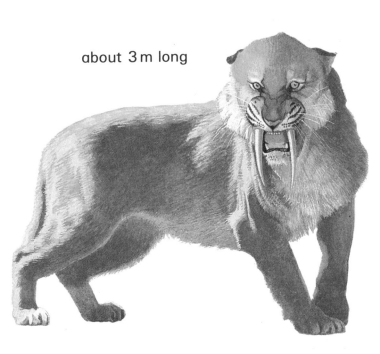

about 3 m long

This tiger had front teeth about
30 cm long. It could kill a
mammoth or any other animal.
But the first people hunted the
sabre-toothed tiger until there
were none left.

Index